FAMILY PETS

OUR PET DOG

by Michele Jakubowski
illustrated by Kev Payne

GRASSHOPPER

Tools for Parents & Teachers

Grasshopper Books enhance imagination and introduce the earliest readers to fiction with fun storylines and illustrations. The easy-to-read text supports early reading experiences with repetitive sentence patterns and sight words.

Before Reading

- Look at the cover illustration. What do readers see? What do they think the book will be about?
- Look at the picture glossary together. Sound out the words. Ask readers to identify the first letter of each vocabulary word.

Read the Book

- "Walk" through the book, reading to or along with the reader. Point to the illustrations as you read.

After Reading

- Review the picture glossary again. Ask readers to locate the words in the text.
- Ask the reader: Dogs are Jack's favorite kind of animal. What is your favorite animal? Would you like to have a dog as a pet?

Grasshopper Books are published by Jump!
5357 Penn Avenue South
Minneapolis, MN 55419
www.jumplibrary.com

Library of Congress Cataloging-in-Publication Data

Names: Jakubowski, Michele, author.
Payne, Kev, 1978- illustrator.
Title: Our pet dog / by Michele Jakubowski;
illustrated by Kev Payne.
Description: Minneapolis: Jump!, Inc., 2022.
Series: Family pets
Includes reading tips and supplementary back matter.
Audience: Ages 5-7
Identifiers: LCCN 2021000213 (print)
LCCN 2021000214 (ebook)
ISBN 9781636901985 (hardcover)
ISBN 9781636901992 (paperback)
ISBN 9781636902005 (ebook)
Subjects: LCSH: Readers (Primary)
Dogs–Juvenile fiction.
Classification: LCC PE1119.2 .J3524 2022 (print)
LCC PE1119.2 (ebook)
DDC 428.6/2–dc23
LC record available at https://lccn.loc.gov/2021000213
LC ebook record available at https://lccn.loc.gov/2021000214

Editor: Eliza Leahy
Direction and Layout: Anna Peterson
Illustrator: Kev Payne

Printed in the United States of America at
Corporate Graphics in North Mankato, Minnesota.

Table of Contents

My Dog, Max

Today, we are learning about animals.

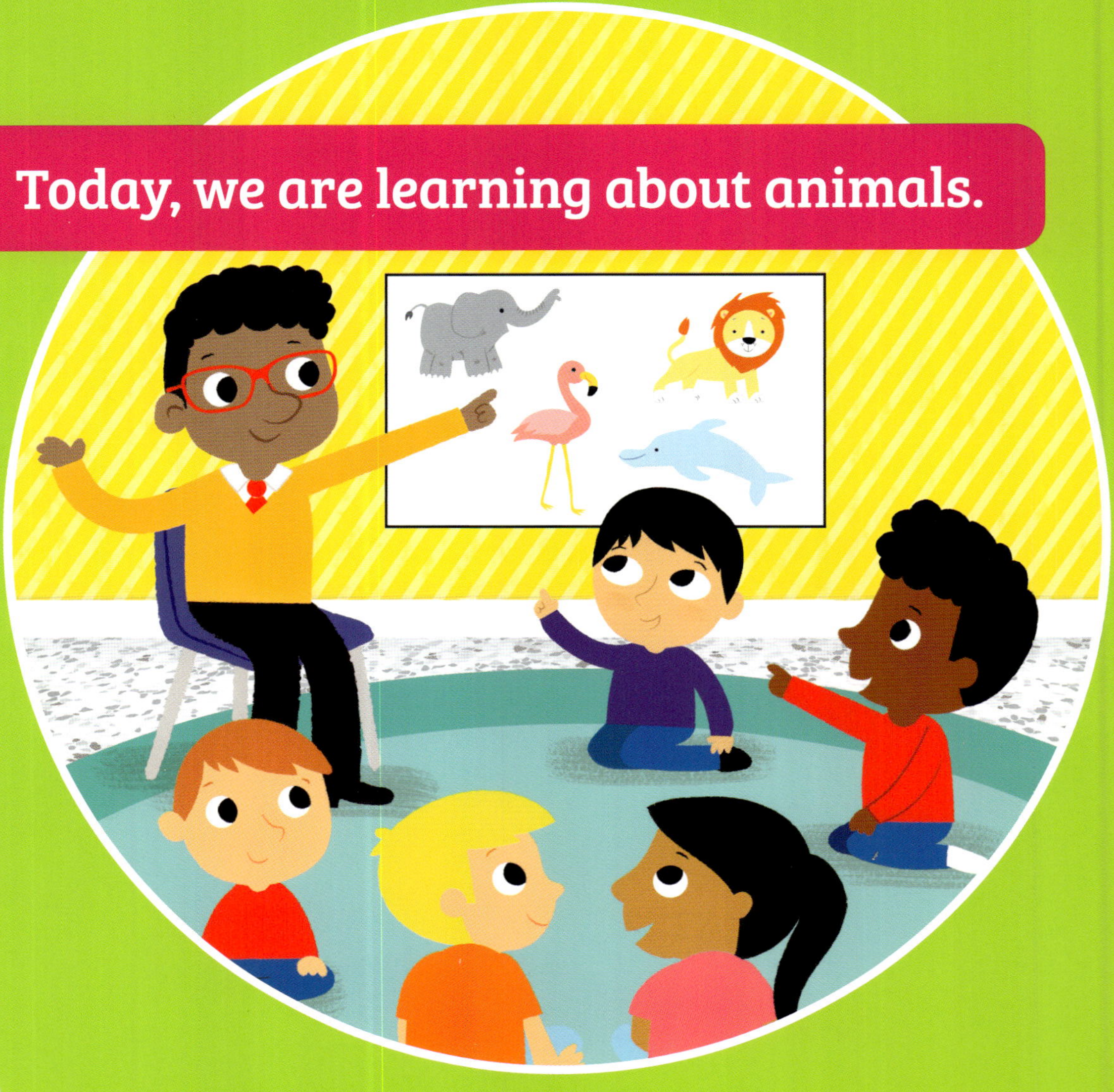

"Jack, what is your favorite animal?" Mr. Alt asks.

"Dogs!" I say. "I have a pet dog. His name is Max."

Max is still a puppy.

He has a lot of energy!

My sisters walk him.

Max wants to run!

We go to the park.

Max wants to play!

I throw the ball for him.

My brother gives Max a bath.

Max shakes off the water!

I fill Max's water bowl.

I feed him kibble.

Max is excited to eat!

At night, Max sleeps
on my bed.

I scratch his ears.

"Good night, Max," I say.

Let's Review!

Everyone had fun at the park! What did Jack and Max play with?

A. a ball **B.** a frisbee **C.** a bone **D.** a rope

Picture Glossary

energy
The ability or strength to do things without getting tired.

excited
Very eager and interested.

kibble
Dry food for dogs.

scratch
To lightly scrape with your fingernails.

Let's Review! Answer Key: **A.** a ball